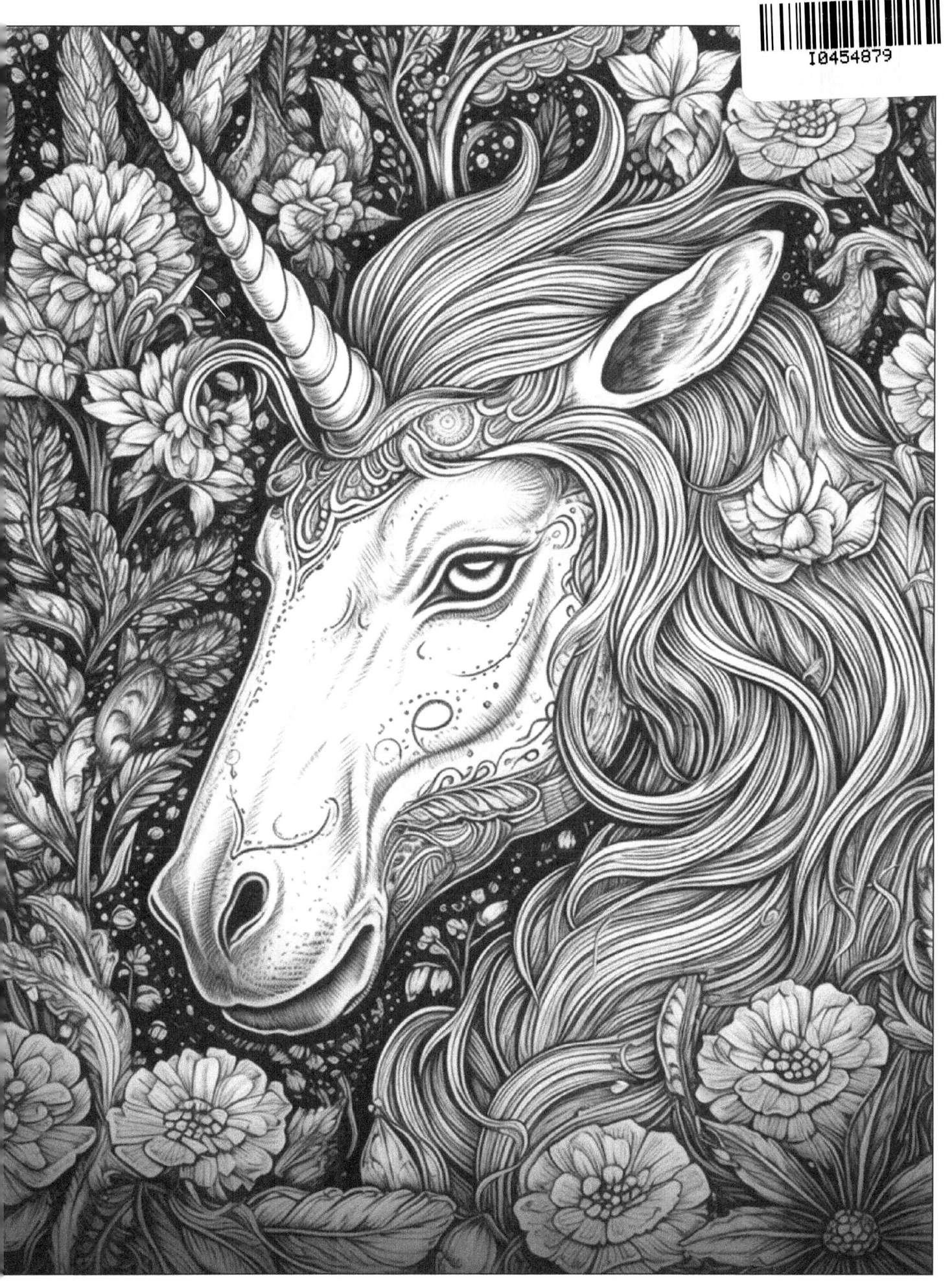

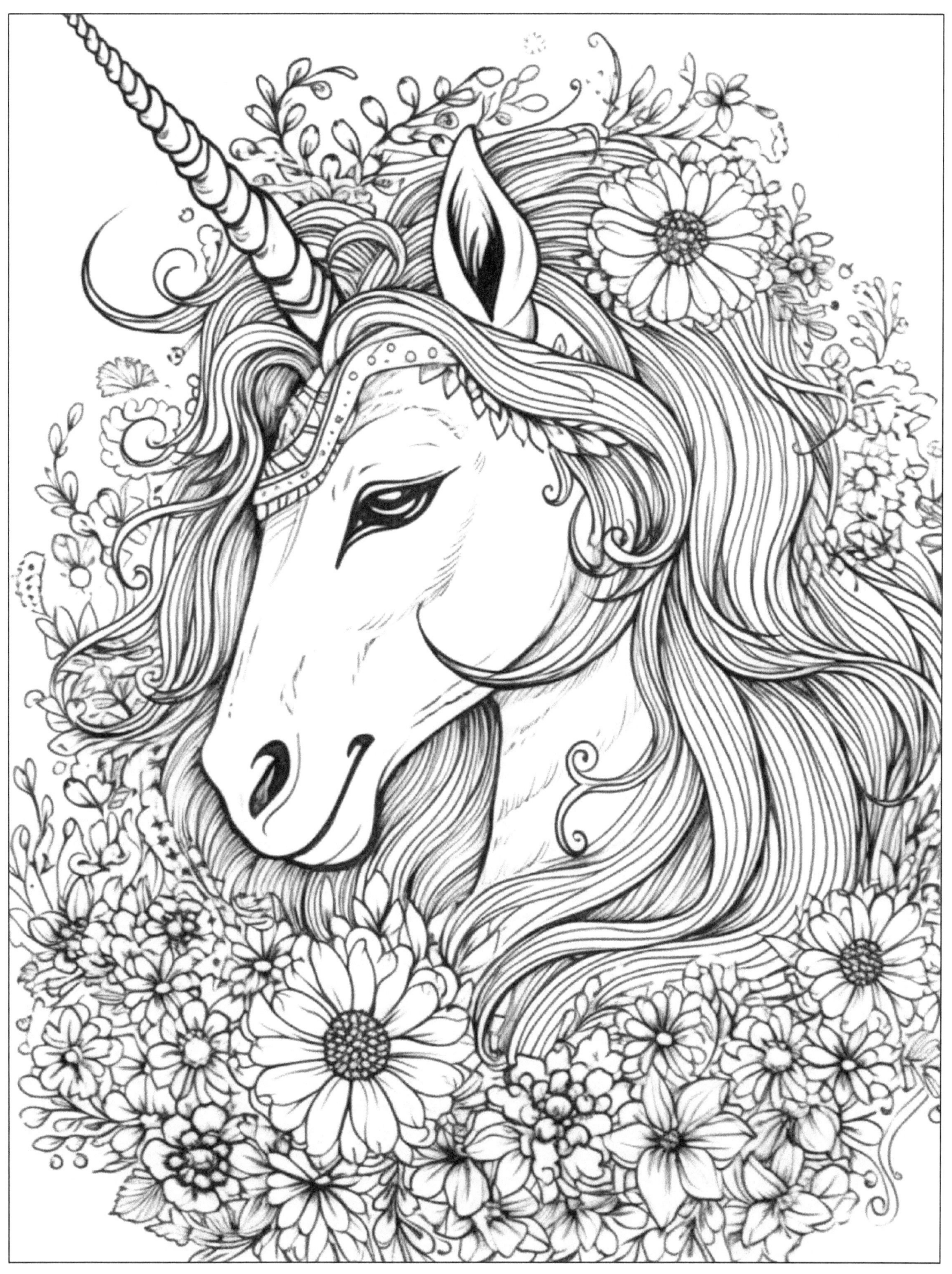

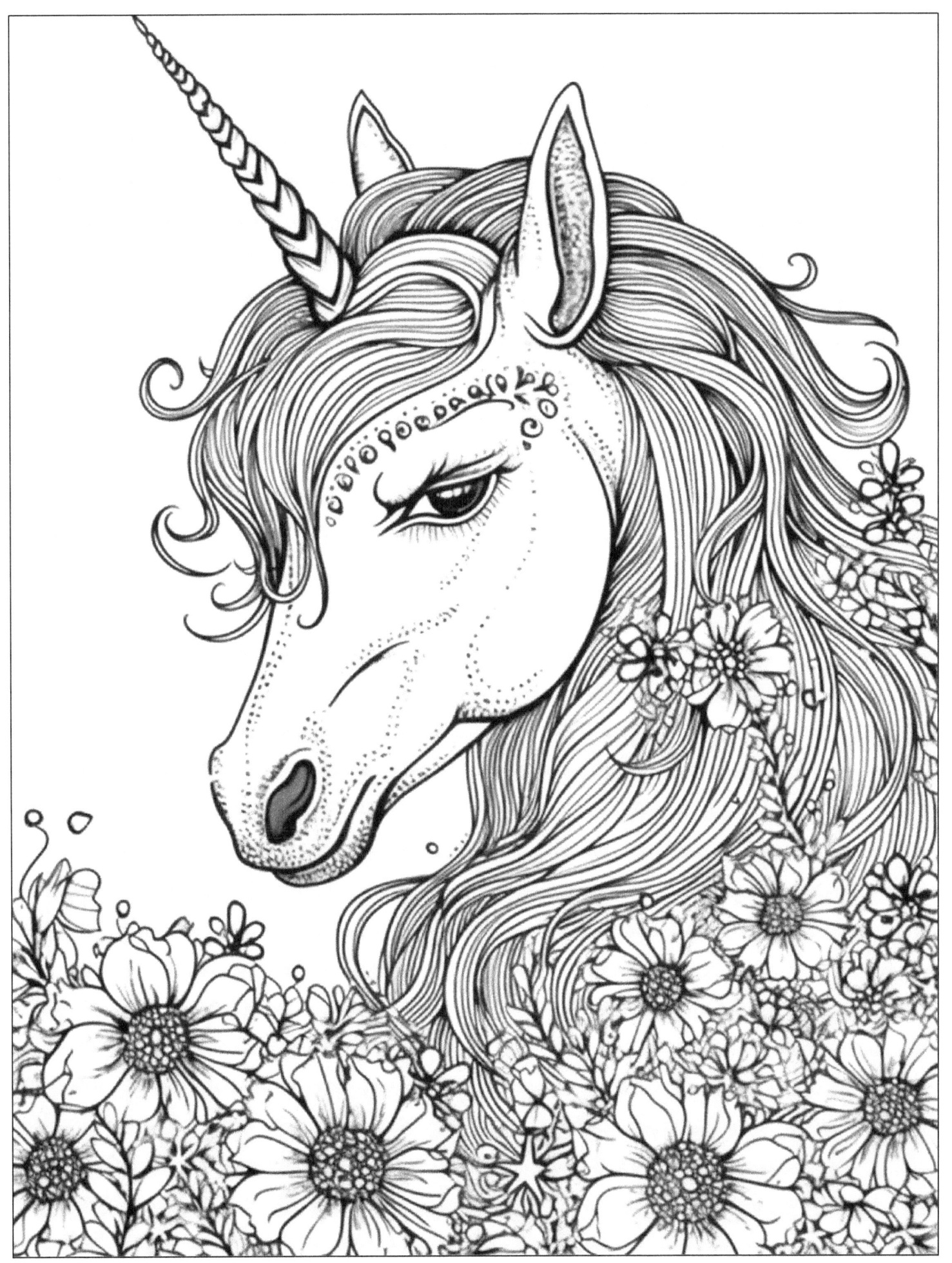

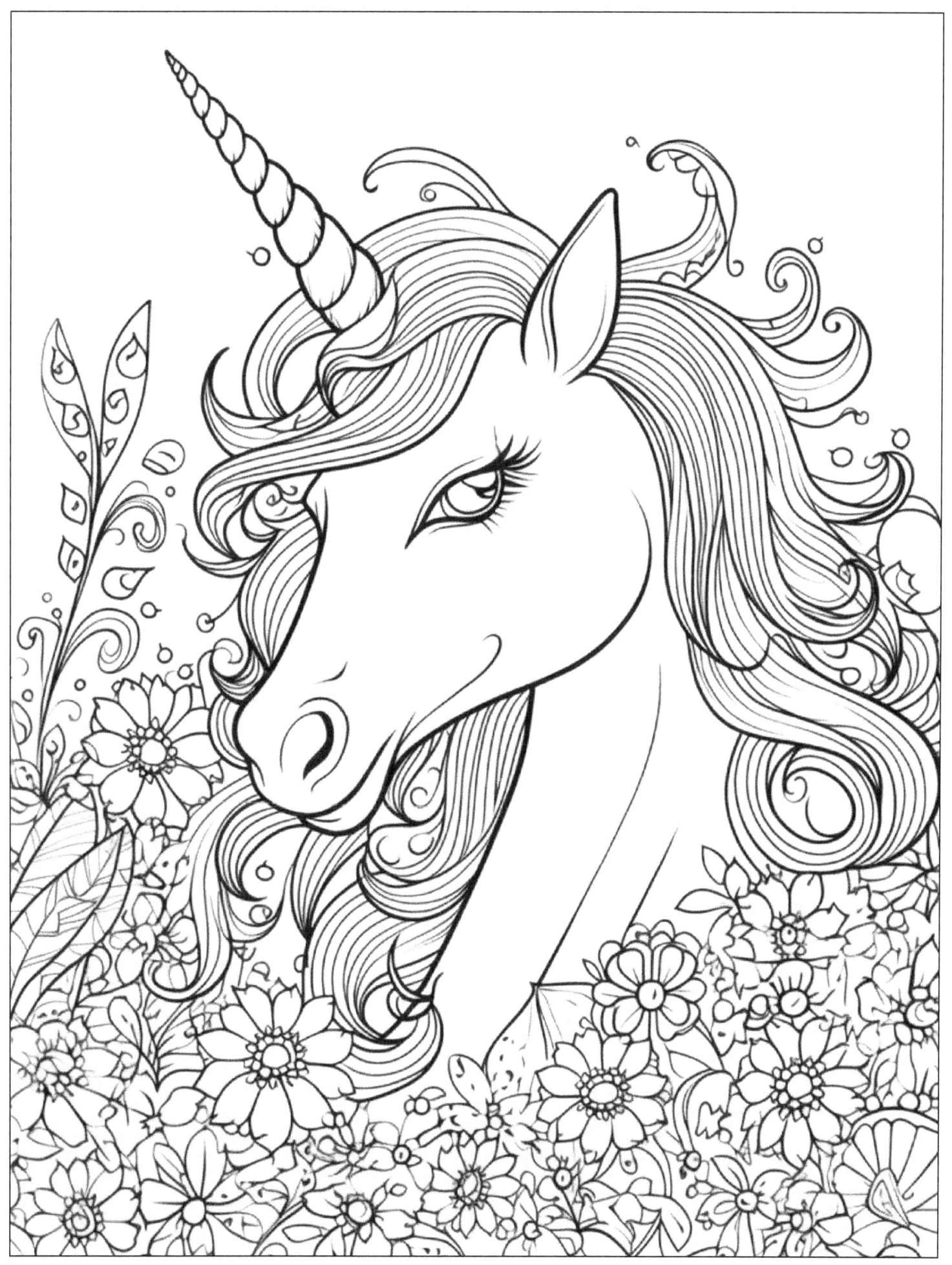

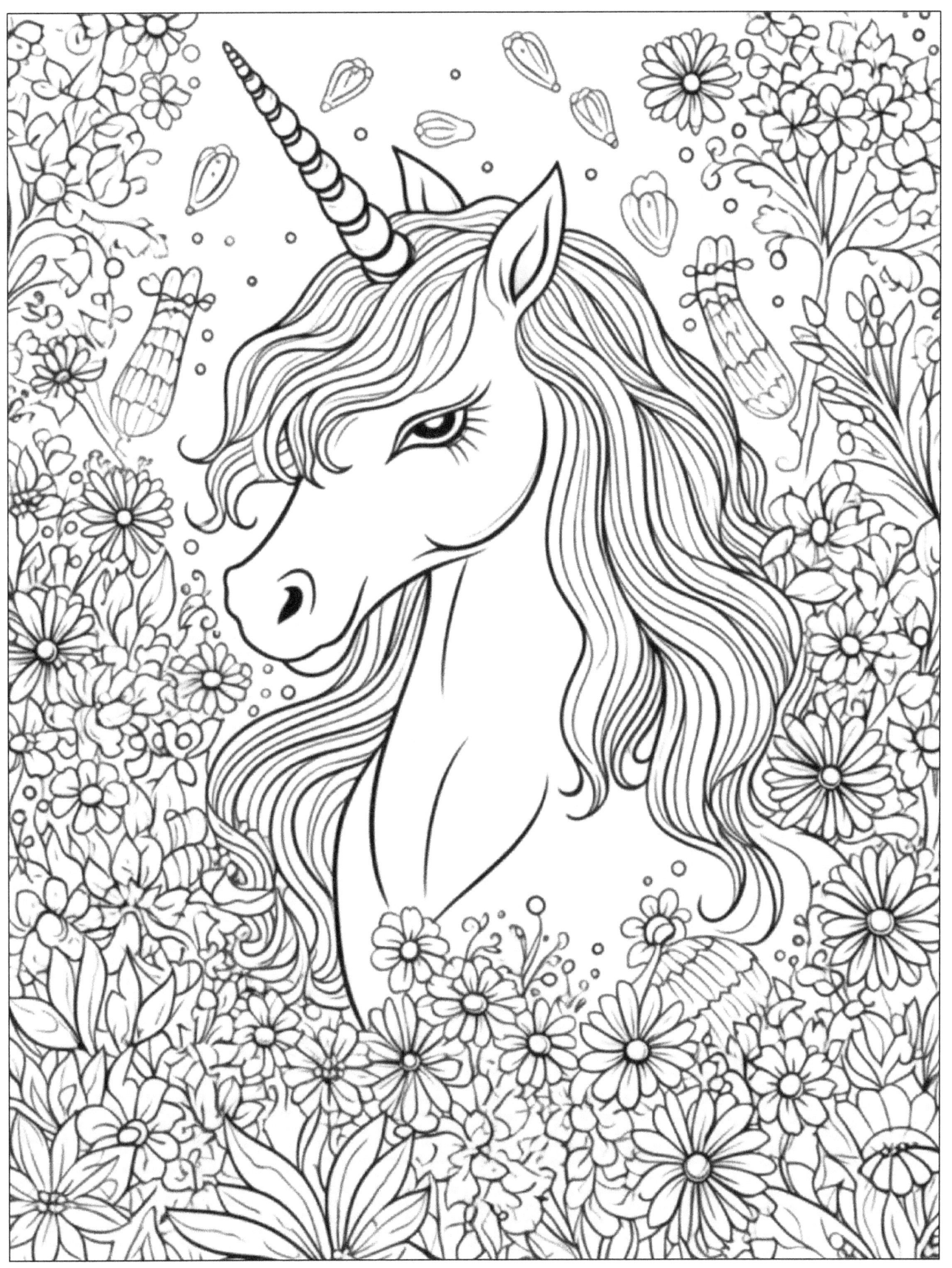

ColorQuest Collections

Fun and creative coloring books for all ages

For more fun and creative coloring books, search for ColorQuest Collections in your favorite bookstore!

www.ingramcontent.com/pod-product-compliance
Lightning Source LLC
Chambersburg PA
CBHW060530010626
45794CB00023B/3127